PREFACE

To fully understand the development of Africa and its present-day turmoil, one must know the history of this magnificent continent, which is four times the size of the United States and three times the size of Europe. At one time, long before Europe emerged from the dark ages, Africa was the pillar of advanced technology and superior civilizations. African kingdoms such as Ghana and Mali, and cities such as Jenne and Timbuktu were the mecca of intellectual centers which boasted mathematicians, astronomers, architects, physicians, jurists, and great material riches (gold, silver, ivory, salt, etc.). African civilizations charted the stars, built the pyramids, created written languages, established the calendar as we now know it, and developed networks of world trade as early as 4000 B.C. In fact, most historical experts recognize Africa as the "cradle of humanity."

Tribal wars and the lucrative slave trade are the primary reasons that brought about the depopulation and downfall of the great, ancient African states. It is documented that the Afro-European slave trade began in 1441, at the hands of the Portuguese. And, it was not long thereafter that the Portuguese were joined by the Spanish, French, Dutch, and English as slave traders. In 1619, the first slaves were reported in English America. The participation of countries in the African slave trade became so profitable that slaves were viewed as "black gold" and beasts of burden. Europeans established trading posts along the West African coastline where beads, guns, whiskey and ivory were bartered for African slaves.

This booklet, *A Salute to Historic African Kings & Queens*, the sixth in a series of Black history publications by Empak Publishing Company, gives an overview of twenty-four significant Black rulers of ancient Africa, and an insight into their respective kingdoms. These notable African kings and queens, whose stories are organized herein according to dates of their reigns, played a major role in Africa's progress and majesty.

Ancient Africa was as varied as its terrain, encompassing peoples and cultures more distinct than any other continent. Thirteen different empires, nations, or kingdoms are represented by the emperors, empresses, kings, and queens whose biographies are presented herein. These thirteen cultures have distinct histories and traditions, yet they are interrelated. Islam and Christianity competed with their ancient beliefs—and with each other; the desire for greater power and wealth caused many of these nations to conquer each other; and the onslaught of the slave traders brought about the loss of a tremendous amount of human and natural resources and the systematic rape of a continent whose peoples had sustained their own identities, borders, trading networks, and languages. This exploitation, which is brought out in some of the biographies, was not met with passive resistance; in many cases, African monarchs led their people into battle against the invasions from outsiders. Throughout the ages, these and other Africans have withstood the challenges of time, nature, and human foibles, and they remain a proud race of people with a fascinating history.

Empak Publishing Company is hopeful that this booklet—*A Salute to Historic African Kings & Queens*—will give Black Americans a more in-depth understanding, appreciation of, and linkage to their origin and history. Black America has every reason to be proud of its rich, vibrant African heritage.

Empak Publishing Company

"A SALUTE TO HISTORIC AFRICAN KINGS & QUEENS"

Published by Empak Publishing Company
212 East Ohio Street, Chicago, IL 60611.

Publisher & Editor: Richard L. Green
Assoc. Editor: Phyllis W. Ragsdale, Mary C. Lewis
Researcher: Phyllis W. Ragsdale, Ted Evans
Production: Dickinson & Associates, Inc.
Illustration: S. Gaston Dobson

CONTENTS

MAP OF AFRICAN KINGDOMS 4
BIOGRAPHIES:*
Menes (fl. c. 3100 B.C.-3038 B.C.) 5
Tuthmosis III (1504 B.C.-1450 B.C.) 6
Hatshepsut (1478 B.C.-1457 B.C.) 7
Akhenaton (fl. c. 1379 B.C.-1362 B.C.) 8
Nefertiti (fl. c. 1379 B.C.-1362 B.C.) 9
Tutankhamon (1361 B.C.-1351 B.C.) 10
Makeda (fl. c. 960 B.C.-930 B.C.) 11
Piankhi (753 B.C.-713 B.C.) 12
Taharqa (688 B.C.-662 B.C.) 13
Massinissa (fl. c. 202 B.C.-148 B.C.) 14
Jugurtha (118 B.C.-106 B.C.) 15
Dahia al-Kahina (fl. c. 667 A.D.-702 A.D.) 16
Gudit (937-977) 17
Mansa Musa I (1312-1337) 18
Sunni Ali Ber (1464-1492) 19
Askia Muhammad (1493-1528) 20
Affonso I (1506-1543) 21
Nzingha (1623-1663) 22
Osei Tutu (1695-1717) 23
Shaka (1813-1829) 24
Moshesh (fl. c. 1824-1870) 25
Yaa Asantewa (1863-1923) 26
Menelik II (1889-1913) 27
Haile Selassie (1930-1974) 28
TEST YOURSELF 29
CROSSWORD PUZZLE 30
WORD SEARCH 31
QUIZ & GAME ANSWERS 32
GLOSSARY .... inside back cover

***Dates shown indicate the period of a ruler's reign.**

Editor's Note: Due to this booklet's space limitations, some facets on the lives of the above noted Historic African Kings & Queens have been omitted.

MAP OF AFRICAN KINGDOMS

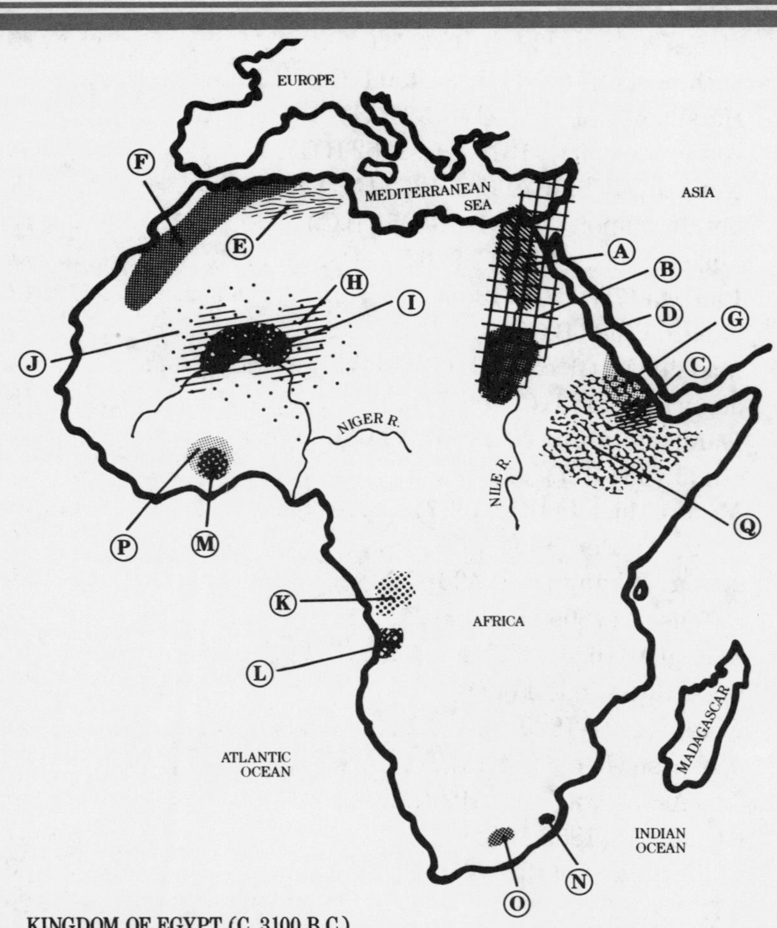

- (A) KINGDOM OF EGYPT (C. 3100 B.C.)
- (B) EGYPTIAN EMPIRE (C. 1500–1300 B.C.)
- (C) KINGDOM OF SHOA (C. 950 B.C.)
- (D) NUBIAN KINGDOM (C. 720 B.C.)
- (E) KINGDOM OF NUMIDIA (202 B.C.)
- (F) BERBER KINGDOM (C. 660 A.D.)
- (G) KINGDOM OF AXUM (C. 970)
- (H) MALI EMPIRE (C. 1330)
- (I) SONGHAY EMPIRE (1475)
- (J) SONGHAY EMPIRE (1497)
- (K) KINGDOM OF CONGO (1540)
- (L) KINGDOM OF NGOLA (1660)
- (M) ASHANTI EMPIRE (1700)
- (N) KINGDOM OF ZULU (1830)
- (O) KINGDOM OF BASUTO (1856)
- (P) ASHANTI EMPIRE (1890)
- (Q) KINGDOM OF ETHIOPIA (1950)

MENES
(Mens)
(fl. c. 3100 B.C.–3038 B.C.)

The first pharaoh of the united kingdoms of Upper and Lower Egypt was Menes or Aha Mena. According to the Palarmo Stone (an important source of historical information for the first four Egyptian Dynasties), the African King Menes decisively defeated the Asian invaders and went on to unite Egypt in approximately 3100 B.C. The boundaries of the kingdoms of Lower and Upper Egypt were never clearly defined, although Lower Egypt appears to have consisted primarily of the Delta and the area immediately south, while Upper Egypt comprised the remainder of the country to the first cataract (waterfall) of the Nile River.

After defeating the northern kingdom, Menes referred to himself as "King of Upper and Lower Egypt," a title that was retained by succeeding pharaohs for thousands of years. Menes' rule began Dynasty I which consisted of five kings and is one of the three dynasties that make up the Early Dynastic Period which flourished from about 3100 B.C. to 2613 B.C.

The basis for the pharaohs' chronology is the *Lost History of Egypt*, by Manetho, a learned Egyptian priest. Manetho's list divides the Egyptian rulers into thirty dynasties, and modern historians have grouped the dynasties into the following sub-divisions: the Early Dynastic Period; the Old Kingdom; the First Intermediate Period; the Middle Kingdom; the Second Intermediate Period; and the New Kingdom Period.

According to the African concept of kingship the pharaoh was not a mortal, but a god made in man's image. He was the bridge between the divine forces and his subjects. The efficacy of the pharaoh's powers maintained his people while he ruled, and also helped to sustain them from his tomb. These attributes were adopted by Egypt's kings following the reign of Menes.

Although modern historians find Manetho's list inadequate, they do not have sufficient documentation to rearrange the list. In many cases, the relationships between the various rulers and dynasties are either uncertain or unknown. Furthermore, many of the dates of accession are subject to questioning.

In addition to uniting Egypt, Menes is also credited with founding the ancient city of Memphis which was located between the two kingdoms. Because of its central location, Memphis was one of Egypt's leading cities, and it served as the capital for a considerable period of time. The city was named after Menes, and its ruins lie not far from present-day Cairo.

Despite our limited knowledge of Menes, his contributions to world civilization have been of considerable importance. The political unification of Egypt played a significant role in the social and cultural development of Egypt. Governmental and social institutions were also developed during Menes' reign, which endured with comparatively little change for almost two millennia. Furthermore, hieroglyphic writing developed immensely during this period, as well as technical skills and other arts. Egypt went on to become one of the most advanced nations in the ancient world and set records of achievement that few civilizations can rival. Menes' dates of birth and death are uncertain, but it is documented that he came from Thinis, a small town in southern Egypt. According to Manetho, Menes reigned for sixty-two years, and he was killed by a hippopotamus.

Despite the scarcity of our knowledge of Menes, history has recorded and time has demonstrated that great civilizations rarely achieve under an inept leader, nor are countries able to retain and consolidate their power without able leadership. Since Egypt was one of the greatest civilizations of all time, it is quite possible that both time and history will render Menes the most influential ruler in the history of humankind.

TUTHMOSIS III
(Tuth-moh'-sis)
(1504 B.C.–1450 B.C.)

Menkheperre Tuthmosis III was the son of Tuthmosis II and a lesser wife. Upon the death of his father, he ascended the throne in 1504 B.C. at the approximate age of ten. For twenty years, his stepmother/aunt, Queen-Pharaoh Makare Hatshepsut, served as his co-regent. The dates of Tuthmosis III's reign are variously provided by different historians, Egyptologists, and anthropologists. Although Tuthmosis theoretically ruled co-regently with Queen Hatshepsut, most documentation lists his dates of reign from the time he ascended the throne as a child in 1504 B.C. until his death in 1450 B.C.

Tuthmosis III was one of the kings of the New Kingdom Period and a member of the Eighteenth Dynasty, the last period of Egyptian greatness, in which the ancient empire reached its zenith. This period was marked by the establishment of a legal code, the building of magnificent temples, and the great military conquests of Tuthmosis III. The Eighteenth Dynasty is the greatest of all Egyptian dynasties and Tuthmosis III is considered by many as its greatest pharaoh.

Although Tuthmosis' mummy proves him to have been a small man in stature (he was less than five feet tall), he was one of the greatest conquerers in history. Napoleon of France has been aptly compared to the Egyptian ruler. As soon as Tuthmosis III assumed sole power, he set off immediately on the first of many military campaigns. Tuthmosis III personally conducted eighteen military campaigns in twenty years, and he was best known for his conquest of southwestern Asia.

During Tuthmosis III's first military encounter, he defeated the Assyrian rulers at Megiddo and successfully besieged that city. The Battle of Megiddo was the first war in history to be recorded in detail. The spoils from this victory included approximately 2,000 Assyrian horses, 900 war chariots, 2,000 Asiatic bulls, 2,000 cattle, and 20,000 other animals. Approximately 2,000 prisoners-of-war were taken, including Assyrian princes and princesses.

The climax of Tuthmosis III's career came when he crossed the Euphrates River and defeated the Mitannians, his principal adversaries, on their own soil. Tuthmosis III then recrossed the Euphrates and erected a stele (monument) beside that of his grandfather (Tuthmosis I), which marked the eastern point of his empire. He erected other such monuments throughout his empire. One of the granite structures, from Heliopolis, is now located in Central Park in New York and its twin rests on the bank of the Thames River in England. Tuthmosis III also fought in Libya and Ethiopia. His campaigns to the South brought Nubia (an ancient region of northeastern Africa) under his control. His conquests brought Egypt an abundance of riches and hordes of captives, which were used as slaves. Tuthmosis' later victories were little more than military parades.

To ensure his son's succession to the throne, near the end of his reign, Tuthmosis III made his twenty-year-old son his co-ruler. A year later, the warrior-king was dead. "Lo, the King completed his lifetime of many years, splendid in might, in valor and triumph," said one of his grieving generals. Tuthmosis III, the world's first great military figure, left his legacy to ancient Egypt by leaving her all that he surveyed. He joined his forebears in the Valley of the Kings.

Over three thousand years later, in 1831, the Pharaoh's tomb was discovered by grave-robbers, along with thirty-six of Egypt's most famous kings and queens. King Tuthmosis III's mummy was taken to the Cairo Museum.

HATSHEPSUT
(Hat-shep'-soot)
(1478 B.C.–1457 B.C.)

The story of Queen Hatshepsut (who later became pharaoh) is one of the most interesting and dramatic incidents in ancient Egyptian history. It is the story of a queen-mother who stole the throne from a child-pharaoh in a coup d'etat and went on to proclaim herself as pharaoh. Hatshepsut ruled Egypt for twenty years in an uneasy peace, until the child-pharaoh grew into adulthood, became Tuthmosis III and presumably destroyed her.

Hatshepsut's story has been referred to as the "Feud of the Tuthmosids" by historians. The saga begins with little Princess Hatshepsut, the only surviving daughter of Pharaoh Tuthmosis I and his royal wife and Tuthmosis II's only son by a lesser wife. When Tuthmosis I became ill, he married Princess Hatshepsut to her half-brother, Tuthmosis II. It was customary for royal brothers and sisters to marry each other in Egyptian culture to preserve royal bloodlines and to keep the throne in the family. When her father died, Hatshepsut's husband became Pharaoh Tuthmosis II and she became queen. Her husband had a son by a commoner, and the royal couple had two daughters. When the boy was about ten years old Tuthmosis II became gravely ill. Before his death, Pharaoh Tuthmosis II married his daughter by Hatshepsut to his son; he later ascended the throne as Tuthmosis III, while Hatshepsut's daughter became queen. Hatshepsut was relegated to queen-mother and co-regent of the boy-pharaoh.

For several years, Hatshepsut, who was approximately twenty years old, appeared to step aside. On state occasions, she walked submissively behind the boy-pharaoh, Tuthmosis III. Apparently to rule co-regently, in the name of the young Tuthmosis III, did not prove satisfactory to Queen-Mother Hatshepsut; she wanted more. History does not detail exactly when or how, but one day in a bloodless seizure of power, Hatshepsut became the first female pharaoh in Egyptian history. She wholeheartedly believed by blood and birth that she was entitled to the throne. First, she claimed that her father Tuthmosis I had always destined her for the crown. She also maintained that she was sired by the ancient sun-god, Amon-Ra. Hatsepsut went so far as to order prints made portraying Amon-Ra coupling with her mother and depicting herself breastless and in male attire.

To immortalize herself, Hatshepsut ordered two obelisks to be quarried at Aswan. The quarrying, transporting and erecting of these monuments represented remarkable achievements in engineering and reflect the considerable amount of control she exercised over Egypt's resources of manpower, equipment, and materials. The needle-like structures were about one hundred feet high and were covered in gold and silver. Hatshepsut's rule was further marked by construction projects of her beautiful mortuary temple and the refurbishing of the many other temples in need of repair. Hatshepsut continued her father's policies, strengthening defenses and improving the economy by restoring foreign trade. Reportedly, Hatshepsut personally led campaigns into Nubia to secure Lower Egypt. During her reign, there were four major, successful military campaigns.

During Hatshepsut's twenty-one year reign, from 1478 B.C. to 1457 B.C., she ruled Egypt well. Her greatest accomplishments were in trade, art, and architecture. Upon the death of her daughter, Hatshepsut designated her stepson/nephew, Tuthmosis III, as her heir and issued him full control over the military. Hatshepsut's end came prematurely and mysteriously. Some say she died a normal death, while others believe that Tuthmosis III seized the throne and killed her. However, Tuthmosis did attempt to destroy her memory by obliterating her name and systematically destroying her monuments after her death. According to Egyptologist James Henry Breasted, Queen Hatshepsut was "The first great woman in history of whom we are informed."

AKHENATON
(Ah-ken'-na-ton)
(fl. c. 1379 B.C.–1362 B.C.)

Amenhetop IV, better known as Akhenaton or Ikhnaton, was renowned for instituting monotheism in Egypt by dictating that his kingdom worship the sun-god, Aton. Aside from religion, his visionary beliefs sparked revolutionary changes in Egyptian art, architecture, and literature. Akhenaton's approximate dates of reign, from 1379 B.C. to 1362 B.C., were known as the Amarna Age.

Amenhetop IV was the great-grandson of the world's first military giant, Tuthmosis III, and the son of Amenhetop III and Queen Tiy. It is generally accepted that he was born in 1393 B.C. Very little is known about his childhood. The beautiful Queen Nefertiti was his wife, and some historians believe that Tutankhamon, his successor, was his son.

At the approximate age of twenty-three, Prince Amenhotep was named co-regent to his ailing father, Amenhotep III. In a great coronation ceremony celebrated near Thebes, the young prince was crowned Amenhotep IV. In the sixth year of his reign, Amenhotep IV established the worship of Aton as the state religion for both citizens and subjects of the Egyptian Empire. The temples honoring the other deities were closed and their statues destroyed. Their names were erased from temples, statues and tombs alike. The name of Amon (also called Amen or Amun) was particularly banned, and whoever bore a name compounded with that of Amon was required to change it. The king himself was the first to do so. He abandoned the name Amenhotep ("Amon Is Satisfied"), and henceforth was known as Akhenaton ("He Who Is Beneficial to Aton"). Even the name of his father, Amenhotep III, was removed from monuments and statues. Akhenaton moved the capital of Egypt from Thebes to Amarna, the site of the modern city of Tel el-Amarna.

Aton was symbolized by paintings of the sun, from which rays descended upon the earth, and each ray ended with an "ankh," the Egyptian symbol of life. The rituals were simple. At sunrise, the royal family gathered for services, while a choir played. There was a second ceremony when Aton reached its zenith and another one at sunset. Akhenaton wrote some of Egypt's most beautiful hymns for the ceremonies.

Once Akhenaton moved to the new capital, he dedicated most of his time to his family, development of the new capital city, and Aton. At that time, he delegated most governmental matters to his administrators. Akhenaton also concentrated his efforts on implementing a new form of art. He personally instructed his artists in the rudimentary use of perspective. Akhenaton insisted that the royal family be portrayed as they really were. Further, unlike his successors, Akhenaton made public appearances, and he drove through the streets unprotected. Exposing the Royal Family to public scrutiny was reportedly criticized by his fellow countrymen.

Akhenaton practiced what he preached. He encouraged respect for women and provided examples by making his mother, his wife, and his six daughters the loves of his life. His was not a violent monarchy. Akhenaton's art failed to show slaves bound in chains or battles led by him. Akhenaton also refused to attack vassal nations and he stated that these regions were free from Egyptian domination. His religious reforms and his loss of Egyptian possessions alienated his people and caused internal conflicts. In the last years of his reign, they referred to him as "the criminal." Upon his death, his religious and artistic innovations were destroyed. Akhenaton died at the age of thirty-one. His exact burial place is uncertain.

NEFERTITI
(Nef-fer-te'-te)
(1379 B.C.–1362 B.C.)

Nefertiti, whose name means "the beautiful one has come," may very well have been short-changed by many historians who stressed only her physical attributes. Nefertiti was the daughter of Ay, a nobleman who was the brother of Queen Tiy. Nefertiti was addressed by her people as "Ruler of the Nile," "Daughter of Gods," and "Empress of the Mediterranean." According to contemporary archaeologists, Queen Nefertiti, wife of Pharaoh Akhenaton, may very well have wielded the major political and religious power of her day. If this is in fact so, Nefertiti was influential in establishing what was perhaps the world's first monotheistic religion, the worship of the sun-god Aton.

Archaeologists state that evidence confirms Nefertiti's preeminence during her husband's reign. They point to the fact that temple carvings of Queen Nefertiti dominated those of Pharaoh Akhenaton. Never in the history of ancient Egypt had a temple in the country's capital emphasized a woman over the king. This is a very strong indication, according to comtemporary historians, that Nefertiti matched her husband in religious stature. Nefertiti was the only queen addressed in prayers and therefore was accorded divinity while her husband was still alive.

Further, inscriptions on stone panels indicate that Nefertiti had ideas of her own regarding possible locations for the new capital that was built by Akhenaton. Archaeologists further confirm that never before in Egyptian history has there been a recorded concession where a queen expressed ideas different from those of the Pharaoh. Some portraits of Nefertiti show her wearing the pharaoh's crown, and some historians have concluded that upon Akhenaton's death, Nefertiti assumed the role of Pharaoh Smenkhkare, who reigned briefly after Akhenaton and prior to Tutankhamon.

On a familial note, Nefertiti was the mother of six daughters, and for several years, she cared for Tutankhamon. During her husband's reign, the royal family set an example of natural family life. The royal couple kissed and embraced their children in public, and they took them riding through the streets. They were depicted in many informal scenes. Queen Nefertiti and her daughters made many appearances from the royal balcony. Despite the closeness between Nefertiti and Akhenaton, he had at least one other wife. Some historians suggest that Tutankhamon may have been the offspring of King Akhenaton by the lesser wife Kiya.

One of Nefertiti's daughters, Ankhesenamon, was the wife of King Tutankhamon. Upon the death of Tutankhamon, Ankhesenamon was determined to hold the throne herself, and as such she considered marrying the son of the King of the Hittites. However, the prince died enroute to Egypt. In addition to Ankhesenamon, another one of Nefertiti's daughters ascended the throne.

It is suggested that after the twelfth year of Akhenaton's reign, Nefertiti apparently was out of grace with the king. Consequently, she lived in a separate palace, and it appears that she was deprived of her throne and functions as the royal wife. No matter how dominant Nefertiti's personality was, she apparently had no desire to upstage her husband, and whatever power she may have wielded was done in a subtle and respectable fashion. Like her husband, Nefertiti's name was stricken from official records and other monuments bearing her name were destroyed by their successors.

Nefertiti's famous life-size bust depicts a beautiful woman and it precisely echoes her praise in an Egyptian hymn as "youthful forever and ever." The bust eloquently speaks to her ageless beauty and was designed by an artist named Tuthmosa (not the pharaoh), which is housed in a museum in Berlin. It is considered one of the artistic masterpieces of all time.

TUTANKHAMON
(Too-tan-kahm'-mon)
(1361 B.C.–1351 B.C.)

Tutankhamon was a young king whose life and reign were brief. He was barely nineteen at the time of his death in 1351 B.C. A small tomb was hastily prepared for him and its contents lavishly improvised. Not long after his death, Tutankhamon's name was removed from the colonnade at Luxor. He "who spent his life making images of gods" faced eternity as though he had never even existed. As fate would have it, some three thousand years later, King Tutankhamon burst from oblivion and rivaled the fame of all other Egyptian pharaohs when his burial chamber was discovered in the Valley of the Kings, with its seals intact.

Tutankhamon was the son-in-law and successor of Akhenaton. Although his origins are obscure, he was most probably a blood relative. Tutankhamon's claim to the throne is based on his marriage to Ankhesenamon, the daughter of Nefertiti and Akhenaton. Prior to his ascension to the throne, he was cared for by Nefertiti and was later taken to Thebes, where his name was changed from Tutankhaton to Tutankhamon, "Living Image of Amon." The name of Aton was removed from both Tutankhamon's and his wife's names.

Tutankhamon was only nine years old in 1361 B.C. when he ascended the Egyptian throne. He was under the influence of Ay, who became his co-regent. Although Ay was an elder statesman, he not only served as the young king's co-regent, but he survived him, officiated at his funeral, and succeeded him as king. It was under Tutankhamon's reign that the capital city was transferred back to Thebes. As such, the "Horizon of Aton" became an abandoned city.

King Tutankhamon described Egypt's conditions prior to his accession as follows: "Now when his majesty appeared as king, the temples of the gods and goddesses from Elephantine to the Delta marshes. . . . had fallen into neglect. . . . The land was topsy-turvy, and as for the gods, they had turned their backs on the land. . . . His majesty made monuments for all the gods. . . . restoring their sanctuaries as monuments. . . ."

Tutankhamon occupied the throne for nine years. He did not live long enough to see his policy of a return to the orthodox traditions of his dynasty take full effect. An examination of his skull suggests that he died from a wound in the region of his left ear, which probably resulted in a cerebral hemorrhage. Perhaps he was wounded in battle or the wound may have been accidental. He left no children to succeed him. However, the two mummified human fetuses that were found in his coffin are believed to have been the remains of his premature infants.

Tutankhamon's small tomb was discovered in the Valley of the Kings in 1922 by Egyptologist Sir Howard Carter. The wooden coffin encased a second coffin, while inside that was still another coffin made of solid gold, which contained the remains of the young king. His mummy was wrapped in linen and decked with jewels. His head was covered with the golden mask of Tutankhamon that was later exhibited at museums around the world. The tomb was also filled with furniture, toys, baby clothes, precious jewels, and numerous mortuary gifts. The treasures of Tutankhamon are considered the most splendid art Egypt has ever produced.

Tutankhamon is famous today chiefly for the sensational discovery of his tomb. However, his principal achievements were the abandonment of the religion of Akhenaton, the restoration of the capital at Thebes, the re-establishment of the worship of Amon, and the other deities that were abandoned under Akhenaton's reign.

MAKEDA
(Ma-kee'-da)
(fl. c. 960 B.C.–930 B.C.)

The legendary Queen of Sheba has been known under various names at different periods. To St. Matthew, she was the Queen of the South. To the ancient Moslems, she was Bilqis. To King Solomon of Israel, she was the Queen of Sheba or Saba. To the ancient Greeks, she was the Black Minerva and the Ethiopian Diana. And to her own people, she was Makeda, the beautiful.

Makeda was the queen of both Ethiopia and Saba, in southern Arabia. It is believed that Axum, the capital city of her empire, was founded one hundred years after the Great Flood. Makeda made many changes and rebuilt the territory of Saba during her reign. There are many versions of the Solomon and Sheba story. This biography is based on the Glory of the Kings, a chronicle of the rulers of Ethiopia.

Queen Makeda was very beautiful and exceedingly rich. She had heard a great deal about the wealth of Israel and the wisdom of King Solomon from her royal merchants. The more she heard the more she longed to travel to Jerusalem. One day she announced to her constituents that she intended to visit Jerusalem to learn from the wise King Solomon. Makeda departed for the Holy City with a caravan of almost eight hundred camels, asses, and mules, which were loaded with precious stones, metals, and other valuable items.

During her six-month visit, Makeda conferred frequently with King Solomon. She was so impressed with his wisdom that she gave up her religion and adopted Judaism. King Solomon desired to father many sons who would rule in the name of the God of Israel. Shortly thereafter, she requested to return to her own country. Although Solomon would have preferred for her to stay, he pulled her aside saying, "Take [this ring] so that thou mayest not forget me. And if it happen that I obtain seed from thee, this ring shall be a sign of it, and if it be a man child he shall come to me. . . ." Queen Makeda promised King Solomon that if she begot a male child, she would crown him king of Ethiopia. At the time of Makeda's reign, Axum and Saba were matriarchies so her promise was significant. The queen departed for home, and nine months and five days after Makeda left King Solomon, she gave birth to a male child. She named him Ibn al-Hakim, "son of the wise man." His royal name was Menelik.

At the age of twenty-two, Menelik traveled to Jerusalem to visit his father. He did not need the ring Solomon had given his mother for identification, because when he arrived in Gaza, the people knew by his appearance that he was Solomon's son. When Menelik finally reached his father, Solomon stated, "He is handsomer than I am, and his form and stature are those of David, my father, in his early manhood." Solomon kissed and embraced his son, and asked him to stay. He promised Menelik the kingdom of Israel upon his death, but Menelik replied, "My lord, it is impossible for me to abandon my country and my mother; I swore to her by her breasts that I would return to her. . . ."

When Solomon realized that he could not persuade his son to remain in Jerusalem, he anointed Menelik king of Ethiopia, bestowed upon him the name of David, and provided him with councilors and officers for the founding of Israel's new kingdom in Ethiopia. Except for a brief period during the ninth and tenth centuries, and until the demise of Haile Selassie, Queen Makeda's descendants have ruled the throne of Ethiopia.

Queen Makeda's tomb, along with twenty-two obelisks of her period, were excavated at Axum in the early 1900's. The reign of Queen Makeda, one of the most beautiful and richest African monarchs, was an important part of East African history and culture.

PIANKHI
(Pe-an'-ke)
(753 B.C.–713 B.C.)

The dream of African rulers recapturing Upper Egypt once again from Asian control may have appeared to be a formidable task. However, King Piankhi of Ethiopia turned that dream into a reality during his reign from 753 B.C. to 713 B.C.

Piankhi, also known as Piye, was a Kushite or Ethiopian who succeeded in unifying Nubia, Meroë, Kush, and Egypt under one empire. The Nubian conquest of Egypt is documented on an obelisk (five feet-ten inches high, six feet wide and sixteen inches thick), which was erected in the temple of Amon by Piankhi. He was the son of Prince Kashat, whom he succeeded. Piankhi regarded himself as king of Kush and Egypt. According to the Egyptian kings' list, Piankhi was the third Kushite ruler of the Twenty-fifth Dynasty of Egypt.

The situation in Egypt just prior to Piankhi's ascending the throne and reaching his objective of unifying Egypt has been aptly compared to that of King Menes of the Archaic Dynasty, well over two thousand years prior. Both King Tefnakhte and Bocchoria, who were of Asian descent, had taken control of the capital city of Thebes and virtually controlled most of the Thebald (Upper Egypt) region.

Piankhi began his royal career as king of Nubia. Each year he regretfully watched as his country paid its annual tribute to Egypt in the form of gold, cattle, soldiers, and other riches. Piankhi decided to end the economic pillage and subjugation of Nubia by the Egyptian rulers of Asian extraction, and consequently set out to conquer Egypt.

Piankhi sailed up the Nile River to Thebes and worshiped in the temple of Amon. He then continued on to besiege Hermopolis where King Namlot surrendered to him. He travelled further up the Nile and captured Memphis and Heliopolis. Piankhi was met by King Osorkon III who also yielded to the Ethiopian monarch. As he continued to sail up the Nile, town after town submitted to him. The entire empire of Egypt was soon in a state of total chaos. Piankhi successfully extended the Nubian kingdom from Napata to the Mediterranean. Like many of his predecessors, he never lived in Thebes. After elevating Nubia to a state of glory, he was content to return to Napata to live.

Aside from his many successful military campaigns, Piankhi is also credited with refurbishing the temple of Amon-Ra. Other than his campaigns and reconstruction projects, little else is known about his forty-year reign and achievements. It is, however, suggested that Piankhi devoted the latter part of his reign to extending his empire to the South.

Piankhi's wife's name was Kenesat, and it is generally acknowledged that his successor, Shabaka, was his younger brother or son. Shabaka found it necessary to undertake the reconquest of Egypt. Piankhi died in 713 B.C. and was buried in a pyramid on the east bank of the Nile River, near the present-day town of Marawi. It is believed that he was buried in a tomb which contained fifteen of his ancestors.

The Twenty-fifth Dynasty holds significance for Black people for several reasons. First of all, it is the only dynasty that European historians and writers officially recognize as being African. Additionally, this period was the last effort on behalf of Blacks to control Egypt. As such, rarely after this period was ancient Egypt ruled by African rulers.

TAHARQA
(Ta-har'-ka)
(fl. c. 688 B.C.–662 B.C.)

Taharqa was one of the Nubian kings that succeeded Piankhi and founded the Ethiopian dynasty which ruled Egypt from approximately 700 B.C., until they were defeated by the Assyrians. During his reign, Taharqa controlled the largest empire in ancient Africa.

Taharqa and the other pharaohs of the Twenty-fifth Dynasty were hailed in Upper Egypt as the rightful rulers of the country, and they were considered successors of the ancient pharaohs. On an obelisk of one of the Assyrian kings, Taharqa is depicted as a Black man.

Taharqa ascended the throne in approximately 688 B.C., at the age of about forty. He was crowned king at Tanis and Thebes, and he reportedly had his mother attend his coronation. Taharqa reigned for about twenty-six years. For slightly over fifteen years, Taharqa fostered economic, religious, and cultural activities in both Egypt and Ethiopia. Trading increased dramatically under his reign.

Taharqa is noted for his construction and cultural projects. He is credited with having a temple carved out of solid granite at Jabal Barkal in the Sudan, and he also built another temple to the gods Osiris and Ptah. A smaller temple was also built at Tanis. In addition to building several temples, Taharqa also had the temple of Mut repaired. In addition to his cultural achievements, it is documented that Taharqa led expeditions as far as the Strait of Gibraltar.

Taharqa was friendly with the Palestinian monarch and was sympathetic toward the Palestinians' conflict with the Assyrians. Although he befriended the Palestinians, Assyrian King Sennacherib did not attempt to invade Taharqa during the beginning of his reign. However, when Esarhaddon became king of Assyria he set out to besiege Egypt. He failed in his first attempt, because his army was destroyed in a sandstorm in the desert. However, on his second attempt he defeated Taharqa and forced him to flee to Memphis. The Assyrians pursued him, but Taharqa managed to escape to the South.

The major cities of the Delta region submitted to the Assyrian king, and consequently, he appointed twenty of them to rule as his vassals. The king then returned to Assyria, and a year later set out to conquer Egypt again, but he died enroute. Upon learning of the king's death, Taharqa immediately expelled the vassal governors, and he later declared himself king of all Egypt.

Ashurbanipal, the newly crowned Assyrian king, set out to destroy Egypt. When Taharqa heard of the king's plan, he retreated to Thebes and finally fled to Kush. During the last years of his reign, Taharqa was associated with Prince Tanutamen, who succeeded him to the throne. One source states that the Nubians might have ruled Egypt indefinitely if they had not interfered with the conflict between Assyria and Palestine.

The descendants of the Kushite Kings ruled in their own country for nearly a thousand years. The Kushite capital was moved from Napata to Meroë in the sixth century B.C. Taharqa was buried in a pyramid at Nuri, and his remains were excavated in 1917 by an expedition sponsored by Harvard University.

MASSINISSA
(Mas-sin-ne'-sah)
(fl. c. 202 B.C.–148 B.C.)

During the third century B.C., several kingdoms flourished in the North African regions that now constitute the sovereign states of Morocco, Algeria, and Tunisia. One of the most influential of these kingdoms was the kingdom of Numidia that was ruled by Massinissa, who was an ally of Rome in the last years of the Second Punic War. Massinissa is best remembered for his economic and political policies.

Massinissa was the son of Gaia, one of the lesser kings of Masaesyli. His mother was a Berber prophetess. Massinissa was born about 238 B.C., and he was educated in Carthage. His brother, Oezalces, was married to the niece of Hannibal, the Carthaginian general.

From 218 B.C. to 202 B.C., Massinissa, while in Spain, fought on behalf of Carthage against the Romans. He then allied himself with Rome and against Carthage. Massinissa's alignment with Rome in 202 B.C. was a decisive step which led to Roman support in his claim to the Numidian throne against Syphax, ruler of the Masaesyli tribe. Numidia was the Roman name for the part of Africa that lies north of the Sahara.

Massinissa's position was strengthened as a result of a clause in the peace treaty of 201 B.C. that brought him territorial gains at the expense of Carthage. As another result of the treaty, Massinissa received some of the war-elephants that were confiscated from Carthage and that he trained and later used in Numidian warfare. Perhaps more importantly, Rome's loyalty was traded throughout his reign when he supplied Rome with provisions during her war with Spain, Greece, and Asia.

Although Massinissa's relationship with Rome and Carthage are well documented, his relations with his rivals in Numidia are less known. However, at the end of his reign, Massinissa had united all of Numidia under his rule. His strongest opponent was Vermina, the son of Syphax, who survived defeat in 203 B.C., and consequently negotiated and secured a peace treaty with Rome in 200 B.C.

Massinissa's primary aim was to build a strong and unified state from the Numidian tribes. To achieve his aim, he introduced Carthaginian agricultural techniques. The Greek historian, Polybius, states that before Massinissa's reign "the whole of Numidia was barren, and considered naturally incapable of bearing cultivated crops. He first, and he alone, demonstrated that it could produce all kinds of cultivated crops." Another source states that Massinissa turned the Numidians into town-dwellers and farmers. Under his reign, the empire of Numidia exported vast amounts of corn to the Mediterranean world.

Massinissa also effected the monetary system of the Numidian economy. Although metal coins were made earlier by both Syphax and Vermina, the bronze and lead coins bearing Massinissa's image were quite numerous, and it appears that they served as circulating currency for the people of eastern Numidia.

Massinissa owned a palace at Cirta, where he threw lavish banquets and parties that were entertained by Greek musicians. He married a Carthaginian socialite who was among his several wives. When he was eighty-six, one of his wives bore him a son bringing his total to well over forty offspring. Some of his sons were provided with a Greek education.

Massinissa led a very active life; at the age of eighty, sources state that he had the agility to jump on his horse and ride bareback. Massinissa died in 148 B.C., at the age of ninety. His kingdom was divided between his three legitimate sons, Micipsa, Gulussa, and Mastanabal. Massinissa designated Micipsa to succeed him.

JUGURTHA
(Jo-ger'-tha)
(118 B.C.–106 B.C.)

Jugurtha was the son of Mastanabal and the grandson of Massinissa, who were Numidian rulers. When his uncle Micipsa died in 118 B.C., Jugurtha and Micipsa's two sons, Adherbal and Hiempsal, inherited the kingdom. Jugurtha usurped western Numidia in 117 B.C. and eastern Numidia in 112 B.C. As a result, war with Rome commenced. Numidia was located just west and south of Carthaginian territory and it later became a Roman province. Consequently, Jugurtha had to contend with Rome for control of Numidia.

The defeat of Carthage in 146 B.C. removed the basis for the friendship between Numidia and Rome. Massinissa was reportedly aggrieved that the Romans had forestalled his own ambition to conquer Carthage, and after his death, his sons were reluctant to support the Roman armies, which were beseiging Carthage. However, friendship between Rome and Numidia was maintained throughout the reign of Massinissa's son, Micipsa. Later, after Micipsa's death, a clash surfaced between his descendants and the Roman Empire.

Micipsa's will stipulated that his kingdom be ruled collectively by Adherbal, Hiempsal, and Jugurtha; if the three survivors could not work together, the kingdom was to be equally divided. However, bickering began immediately. In 117 B.C., shortly before the kingdom was divided, Hiempsal was reportedly murdered by Jugurtha. Fragmentation occurred; the majority of Numidians remained loyal to Adherbal, while a smaller group aligned with Jugurtha.

Adherbal sent a mission to Rome to report his brother's death. Jugurtha also dispatched an emissary to Rome. Consequently, the Romans mediated the dispute over the Numidian throne. They proposed that the empire be divided between the two remaining heirs. Jugurtha was to receive the western portion of the empire, and Adherbal received the eastern section, with Cirta as the capital. The fighting between Adherbal and Jugurtha continued and consequently resulted in Adherbal's death. The Romans considered Jugurtha's action to be contemptuous. Jugurtha blatantly refused to accept the Romans' authority, and after a series of incidents, the situation led to the Jugurthine War. After Jugurtha won several campaigns, a truce was reached in 110 B.C.; however, fighting soon broke out again. As such, Jugurtha began a systematic campaign to sweep the Romans from the Numidian Empire.

In 108 B.C., the Romans sent Metellus as commander-in-chief to take control of the situation in Numidia. That same year, Metellus invaded Numidia and defeated Jugurtha in the Battle of the Muthul. With Marius, a Roman general in command, the Romans then went on to occupy most of the regions in the Numidian Empire.

Jugurtha was still bent upon liberating his kingdom from European domination. He took refuge in the desert and then began another campaign against the Roman invaders. This time, though, he met his final defeat. The Roman general Sulla, determined to capture Jugurtha, executed a plot instigated by Bocchus, a Numidian king who was Jugurtha's father-in-law. Bocchus tricked his son-in-law into appearing before him, and Sulla captured Jugurtha. He was taken to Rome, where he was executed in 106 B.C.

Reportedly, Jugurtha did not want warfare. In fact, one source states that there is every reason to believe that he sought peace. His policy was clear. Having coveted the Numidian throne, he successfully won it, and when he desired to be left in the enjoyment of his gains, he was forced to pay the price for peace. The source further states that it was Rome who insisted on war for the political and economic purposes of controlling the northern part of Africa. In short, Jugurtha and the people of Numidia were forced into the Jugurthine War to defend their own kingdom from European domination.

DAHIA AL-KAHINA
(Da'-hee-ah el Ka'-he-na)
(fl. c. 667 A.D.–702 A.D.)

During the seventh century, the decline of Christianity as a religious and cultural influence in North Africa led to the subsequent rise of Islam. Although some North Africans accepted Islam, many others physically resisted. The heart of this resistance to the Arab invaders were the Berbers, a loosely joined group of nomads and small farmers. One such Berber, Kuseila, fought against the Arab invasion. However, he and his supporters -- which included Byzantine soldiers attempting to sustain the Christian influence -- were defeated in 682 A.D. Upon Kuseila's death, his relative, Queen Dahia al-Kahina, became the guiding spirit of North African resistance to Arab invaders, led by Hassan al-Numan, after the collapse of Carthage. Under the leadership of Queen Kahina, the Arabs were driven northward into Tripolitania. The fierce attacks spearheaded by Kahina made some Arab politicians seriously doubt whether North Africa could be conquered.

Like Queen Gudit of Ethiopia, there is uncertainty about her name, because "Kahina" is supposedly a nickname or surname (meaning "Prophetess") given to her by the Arabs. Some sources state that her first name was Dihya or Dahina. Although there are questions about her actual descent, it is written that at one time she was married to a Greek and that she had two sons, one of Berber descent and one of Greek descent. Some authorities state that Kahina was a Black Hebrew, others say she was a member of a nomadic tribe that had first adopted Judaism, but had afterwards converted to Christianity when the Byzantine Empire spread throughout what is now Morocco, Algeria, and Tunisia. Black contemporary historians clearly state that Kahina was Black.

When Kahina's political career began, she was a widow and supposedly was very old. Legend holds that she lived for 127 years, and for 35 of those years she was Queen of the Aures. After Hassan conquered Carthage and destroyed the Byzantine forces in 682 A.D., he regrouped his army and turned it towards the Aures, Kahina's mountainous homeland. The confrontation took place on the banks of the Oued Nini, in what is now northeastern Algeria. This battle proved to be disastrous for Hassan and was considered his first real military setback. Kahina then ordered that the fertile areas be turned to wasteland in an effort to discourage the Arabs from returning. The devastating effect on the soil can be seen to this day in certain parts of Tunisia. As a result of his defeat, many of Hassan's men were taken as prisoners. Kahina treated them well, one of whom, Khalid Yazid, she cared for and later adopted.

Hassan kept himself informed, alledgedly by Khalid, of Kahina's military strategies and thereupon received reinforcements. In 697 or 698 A.D., Hassan again attacked and he and Kahina clashed. This time it was to Kahina's disadvantage; she fled to the Aures Mountains for refuge. The last battle between Hassan and Kahina took place at Tarfa, and both sides considered it a fight to the death. Regretfully, in 702 A.D., Hassan defeated Queen Kahina in her courageous attempt to save the northern part of Africa from Arab domination. After her death, the Arabs changed their strategy for advancing Islam in the region.

Kahina's energy, bravery, and determination made a considerable impact on African history, and some contemporary historians have compared Queen Dahia al-Kahina to the courageous Joan of Arc.

GUDIT
(Guu'-deet)
(fl. c. 937–997)

Although sources agree that there was a woman who flourished in the tenth century who seized the Ethiopian throne, persecuted members of the Solomonic dynasty, and destroyed monuments and other artifacts at Axum, many of these same sources are not in agreement as to her name, her origin, and her motives. She is variously referred to as Queen Esther, Gudit, Yodit, Judith, and Esato.

According to noted historian E. A. Budge, the Solomonic dynasty, whose members were descendants of King Solomon and the Queen of Sheba, was interrupted in approximately 950, and for about 300 years the throne of Ethiopia was occupied by the Zagwe dynasty. Although the Zagwe ruled Ethiopia from approximately 950 to 1260, many European chroniclers have refused to regard the Zagwe as a monarchy, and consequently have omitted them from the Ethiopian kings' list.

The problem of identifying Gudit is complex indeed. To add to the complexities of correctly identifying this revolutionary ruler, who is credited with destroying the ancient Axum Empire, some historians question if she was in fact a queen. Contemporary Ethiopian, Arabic, and European scholars attribute at least three possible beginnings and interpretations to Queen Gudit. Some historians believe that she was a member of the Zagwe dynasty whose lineage has also been under some historical confusion. Some authorities claim that the Zagwe were descendants of the Solomonic dynasty. If this hypothesis is true, it is interesting to note that authorities have failed to state why Queen Gudit turned on her own people.

Other scholars refute this position. They believe Queen Gudit founded the Zagwe dynasty and that she was in no way related to the descendants of David. These scholars further state that there were eleven Zagwe rulers in all, and that each reigned for approximately thirty years. It is documented that Queen Gudit reigned for almost forty years. Still other historians question both of these hypotheses. This group boldly states that Queen Gudit founded the Falasha dynasty that reigned from 950 to 1260. J. A. Rogers, a noted historian, states that during this period there was a Black Hebrew Queen named Esther that seiged the ancient empire of Axum.

Arabic documentation lends still another interpretation regarding the queen in question. Arabic text states a female ruler (and they fail to mention her name) was a former ruler of the once powerful kingdom of Damot. Arab sources further state that the queen's rebellion represented an attempt by the people of southern Ethiopia to gain their independence and to resist domination by the Semites and Christians. This hypothesis receives much scholarly support.

Historians of African and Arabic persuasion are in agreement on the following facts of the queen in question. They believe there was a woman that flourished in Ethiopia during the tenth century, who was most likely a non-Christian, who destroyed Axum and to whom the transfer of political power further southward can safely be credited. Evidence further supports that this leader not only devastated the countryside, but she also harassed and killed many members of the Solomonic dynasty. Furthermore, most sources document that the woman's name was Gudit and that her Arabic name was "Esato," which means fire. These sources also consider the revolutionary leader to be Queen Gudit.

There is further agreement about the Zagwe dynasty. Although they were condemned as usurpers, they are believed to have long been capable rulers and to have enhanced Ethiopia's rich history with important cultural and religious activities. The dynasty is credited with designing highly decorative churches, in the tradition of Ethiopian "rock" churches, that have been reputed to be among the architectural wonders of the world.

MANSA MUSA I
(Man'-sa Moo'-sa)
(1312–1337)

The Mandingo empire of Mali was one of the three great African empires of the medieval period. Although Mali's history dates back to Paleolithic times, the empire did not reach its zenith until the thirteenth century. Mansa (Emperor or King) Musa I was considered Mali's greatest king, reigning from 1312 to 1337. When Mansa Musa ascended the throne, Mali stretched from the mouth of the Senegal River on the Atlantic Ocean to the eastern bank of the Niger River. To the North, Mali reached deep into the Sahara. During Mansa Musa's reign, Mali expanded considerably. At one point, it was as large as Western Europe.

Mali was an empire of considerable wealth. Its natural resources included silver, gold, copper, and salt. Major crops included cotton, corn, millet, yams, and kola nuts. The lifeblood of the empire were its trade routes. To protect his kingdom, Mansa Musa I had a standing army of over 100,000 and a calvary of 10,000.

During Mansa Musa's reign, Mali was a highly sophisticated political state. Administratively, each province had a governor who was appointed by and accountable to the king. Under each governor was a mayor who administered the cities and leading towns. There were also vassal kingdoms that were not under imperial control. Further, there were several semi-autonomous kingdoms that were in direct alliance with the empire. At its zenith, Mali was so organized and powerful that it spearheaded West Africa's Golden Age.

The people of Mali possessed rare beauty and the most admirable qualities. Not only were the women shown the greatest of respect, but royal lineage was also passed on through the mother's brother. There was complete security from violence, and justice and truth prevailed. During this same period, Europe was coming out of the Dark Ages and was full of robbers, idolators, and war mongers.

Mansa Musa I was a devout Moslem. The most colorful event of his reign was his famous "hajj" (pilgrimage) to Mecca in 1324. The journey to Mecca is one of the five duties of members of the Islamic faith. Some say Mansa Musa's royal caravan consisted of 10,000 travellers, others said there were as many as 60,000. To finance his trip, there were approximately one hundred camels, each of which carried three hundred pounds of gold. By July 1324, Mansa Musa and his entourage reached Egypt, where he received a royal welcome. Gold and other expensive gifts were given freely to the Egyptian officials. One Egyptian diplomat documented that it took Cairo's gold markets nearly ten years to return to normalcy after Mansa Musa's trip. From Cairo, Mansa Musa departed for Mecca.

His pilgrimage prompted European cartographers, in 1374, to publish an atlas showing the location of Mali. The following inscription accompanied the map. "This Negro Lord is called Mansa Musa, Lord of the Negroes of Guinea. So abundant is the gold which is found in his country that he is the richest and most noble king of all the land."

Mansa Musa persuaded Moslem scholars, architects, jurists, and others to return with him to Mali. As a result, the city of Timbuktu became a leading center of Islamic studies, and Arabic architecture was introduced into Mali. Thus, Mansa Musa can be credited with laying the foundation on which Islamic tradition was established in West Africa.

Mansa Musa I died in 1337. With his passing, rivalry for power, competition for wealth, and religious reform movements, led to the decline of Mali.

SUNNI ALI BER
(Soo'-ni Ah'-lee Beer)
(1464–1492)

In 1325 when Mansa Musa was in Mecca, the Malian army invaded the capital city of the kingdom of Songhay and made that city a vassal region of the empire of Mali. To ensure that this newly acquired region remained loyal to Mali, the king's sons, Prince Ali Kolon and Sulaymon Nar, were forced to return to Mali as guest-hostages. After Mansa Musa's death, the sons escaped, returned to their homeland and founded the Sunni dynasty that later challenged the supremacy of Mali. Prince Ali Kolon was none other than Sunni Ali Ber.

Sunni Ali began his political career as a soldier in the army of Kankan Musa, a Mandingo ruler of the Mali Empire. When Sunni the Great ascended the throne in 1464, an age of the greatest achievement began for the Songhay Empire. Although Sunni Ali professed to be a Moslem, he held steadfast to his traditional African religion. Like many of the Moslem kings of the Sudanic region, he subscribed to Islam for purely political and economic reasons. In short, the success of many African kingdoms depended upon cooperating with the Arabs. But when important decisions had to be made, Ali turned to his traditional faith for guidance.

Sunni Ali's twenty-eight year reign was a period of one military campaign after another. He was one of the most skillful warrior-kings of his day. Ali was always at the front, fighting to unite the Western Sudanic region. During his reign, he conducted successful campaigns against the Mossi, Dogon, and Fulani, and in 1469 he drove the Tuareg out of Timbuktu. Sunni Ali Ber was never defeated.

Sunni Ali also desired to capture the cultural, intellectual and commercial center of Jenne, but conquering that city proved to be no easy task. The people of Jenne were brave and equally skilled military strategists, and the city was protected by natural barriers that included a network of waterways and rolling hills. It took Ali seven years to overcome that city; in 1473, Jenne's young ruler finally yielded to Ali. The defeated monarch was surprised at the good treatment he received from Ali; not only was the chief of Jenne treated as an equal, but Sunni Ali did not pillage the city as he did Timbuktu. He was as gracious to the subjects of Jenne as he was ruthless to the nomads and scholars of Timbuktu. He further consummated his victory by marrying the queen-mother of the defeated chiefdom and encouraging intermarriage between the peoples of Mali and Songhay. At the culmination of his reign, Sunni Ali ruled an empire much larger and wealthier than that of the great French ruler Napoleon.

Aside from being a skillful warrior, Sunni Ali was also an astute administrator. He had a cabinet of advisors that consisted of a minister of military and external affairs, a treasurer, justice of the courts, and an administrator of the vassal kingdoms.

In 1483, Sunni Ali Ber initiated a canal-building project that was designed to capture the city of Walata and stronghold of Akil, one of his Moslem adversaries. However, the project was still in the process of being completed when Sunni Ali disappeared. One source states that it is likely that Ali drowned while attempting to cross a rapid stream in a canoe.

Like many of the kings of the West African Sudanic region, Sunni Ali Ber was a military strategist of the highest ability and a capable leader. He was also much more. Although Ali expanded his empire by force, he respected and defended African religiosity and traditions against the Moslem nomads, and in time of need and guidance he reached out to his own faith. For that, Black people everywhere should be both pleased and proud.

ASKIA MUHAMMAD
(As-kee'-ah Mo'-ham-med)
(1493–1528)

Upon the death of Sunni Ali, his son, Bakori Da'a inherited the throne. Like his father, he subscribed to traditional African beliefs. Because Bakori would not convert to Islam, he eventually lost the support of the trading cities, which were the centers of Islamic power. After a year, he was overthrown, and Muhammad Ture, Sunni Ali's chief minister became emperor in 1493, taking the military title of Askia.

Like Sunni Ali, Askia Muhammad reigned for thirty-five years. Under Askia the Great, the empire of Songhay extended eastward over the Hausa States across the northern part of Nigeria, into the Sahara region, and west to the Atlantic Ocean. Songhay became the largest and the most powerful of the West African Empires.

Three aspects of Askia the Great's reign deserve mentioning. Unlike Sunni Ali, he based his power on the trading towns and ruled in accord with Islamic teachings and traditions. Accordingly, his dynasty was replete with professionals, judges, tradesmen, and artists of Islamic persuasion, and Askia sought their advice. To strengthen Islam in his country, Askia the Great restored Ammar as governor of Timbuktu. Ammar had previously governed that city, but he fled when Sunni Ali seiged Timbuktu.

Like Mansa Musa, Askia also made a lavish pilgrimage to Mecca, almost one hundred and fifty years later. Although his hajj did not receive nearly the attention of the ruler of Mali, while he was in Egypt Askia Muhammad was honored by the caliph of Carlo by being appointed as the caliph's personal representative to the Sudanic region.

When Askia Muhammad returned to Goa in 1497, he was strengthened in the Islamic faith, and he considered it his duty to extend his empire in the name of Islam. In an effort to convert the people of Songhay, Askia the Great was victorious in initiating a series of "jihads" (holy wars). Other campaigns were commenced to capture the various trading centers. In 1501, Askia defeated Mali, and in 1513 the Hausa territories became part of his domain. He also conquered a settlement in the northern part of Songhay and that principality had to pay an annual tribute of approximately $150,000. Although Askia was a military leader of the highest ability, his record was not without failure. King Kanta, a ruler of a small kingdom located between the Hausa states and the Niger River, was able to maintain his people's independence.

Aside from being a successful military combatant, Askia Muhammad is also credited with further developing a strongly centralized government. The most important government posts of his dynasty were the treasurer, the chief of tax collection, chief of the navy, chief of forestry and wood cutters, and chief of fishermen.

Songhay also enjoyed a cultural and intellectual rebirth under the leadership of Askia Muhammad. Centers of learning were established in Goa, Jenne and Timbuktu. The curriculum included courses in astronomy, mathematics, medicine, rhetoric, and philosophy. Professor Ahmed Baba, a faculty member of the University of Sankore in Timbuktu, authored more than forty books, and his personal library included 1,600 volumes.

In 1528, after it became known that Askia was weakened by the onset of blindness, one of his sons, Musa, forced him to give up the throne. Then, in 1531, Askia's nephew, Muhammad Mar, ascended the throne and immediately forced Askia into exile, where he remained until 1537, when another one of his sons ascended the throne and freed him. Askia Muhammad died one year later, on March 2, 1538. He was ninety-seven years old.

Askia Muhammad was the complete antithesis of Sunni Ali. While Ali defended traditional African religiosity, under the leadership of Askia the Great the armies of Islam triumphed over the Sudan region. Askia the Great was most likely the most devout Black Moslem king of ancient West Africa.

AFFONSO I
(Af-fon'-so)
(1506–1543)

Mvemba Nzinga, who was baptized Affonso I, ruled as the Mani Congo (King of the Congo) from 1506 to 1543. Having adopted Christianity, Affonso I attempted to strengthen his country by proselytizing and westernizing the Congo. Because the Portuguese were primarily interested in exploitation, his efforts failed.

Affonso I was the son of Nzinga Nkuwu, who received the first Europeans to the Zaire region in 1482. Hoping that his country would benefit from western modernization and education, Nzinga Nkuwu and Mvemba (Affonso) converted to Christianity. Upon his father's death in 1506, Affonso I assassinated his brother, Mpanzu a Nzinga, because of his failure to convert to Christianity, and ascended the throne. King Affonso successfully defeated his brother because he used sophisticated European weaponry that he received from the Portuguese.

At first it appeared that the Portuguese supported Affonso I in his efforts to educate his constituents and modernize his country. Not only did Affonso build several schools, but he also sent his son, Dom Henrique, to Portugal to study and in 1518, Henrique was consecrated as a bishop.

However, it soon became clear that the Portuguese were mainly interested in the economic exploitation of the Congolese. Consequently, Affonso's objective, to revitalize his country, ran into difficulties. Not only were the Portuguese indifferent to King Affonso's request for supplies to modernize his country, but the Portuguese technicians sent to the Congo were lazy and refused to work. Furthermore, since many Portuguese were illiterate, they were unable to formally educate Affonso's people. The Europeans were also immoral and treated the Congolese people with disrespect. Even many of the Christian priests were vulgar, and they conspired against King Affonso and his people.

To make matters worse, it was not long after King Affonso ascended the throne that the Atlantic slave trade began. When the Portuguese first arrived in the Congo, they were anxious to return to Europe with slaves as proof that they had reached Africa. At first the Congolese captives were honored and treated with respect. The first Congolese slaves served the Portuguese as interpreters, informants, and guides. However, as the number of Africans in Europe increased, they were relegated to marginal tasks and were eventually reduced to slaves.

As the situation worsened, King Affonso I wrote a letter to the king of Portugal, demanding that he send an ambassador to the Congo to control the situation. In return for remedying the dilemma, the king of Portugal demanded payment in the form of slaves and precious minerals. Although Affonso I was disturbed about the rise of slavery, he abided by the Portguese's demands--as did many other African kings--so he could maintain trade with Europe. Affonso I attempted to control the slave traffic, but by 1530, at least 5,000 slaves were exported annually from the Congo. As the demand for slaves increased, the Europeans pitted one African king against the other, in an effort to control the slave trade themselves. The situation grew so grave that on Easter Sunday in 1539, a group of Affonso's adversaries attempted to assassinate him.

In about 1543, King Affonso I died after reigning thirty-seven years. Although King Affonso was naive and lacked the political astuteness to effectively deal with the Portuguese, he is remembered as a sincere ruler. It should be noted, however, that some of his decisions led to the decline of the Congo. His violent succession to the throne by assassinating his brother brought about intense rivalries, which later divided the country. Finally, his acts to abolish forms of African religiosity, due to his strong belief in the need to convert his people to Christianity, led to the destruction of many forms of traditional Congolese culture.

NZINGHA
(N-zin'-gah)
(1623–1663)

Nzingha was also known as Jinga, Ginga, and Ann Zingha. The renowned warrior-queen was the sister of King Ngoli Bdoni of Ndongo in what is now known as Angola. Nzingha was born in 1582, and at that time the Portuguese were encroaching upon her territory. She was a member of the ethnic tribe called the Jugas. Upon her advent to the throne in 1623, Nzingha presented the Europeans with their stiffest opposition. Consequently, she led her army against the Portuguese and won battle after battle.

In 1622, Nzingha represented her brother at a peace conference at Loanda with the Portuguese viceroy. The treaty of 1622 was designed partly to eliminate the war in the West-Central region of Ndongo. Nzingha unconditionally refused to accept the alliance as it was originally presented, and she was successful in eliminating tribute payments to the king of Portugal. She emphasized that releasing the Portuguese prisoners of war was concession enough.

While Nzingha was in Loanda, it appears that she embraced Catholicism, was baptized, and adopted some European customs. Upon her return to Angola, her brother died, and in 1623, Nzingha became queen. Her first official duty was to send an ultimatum to the Portuguese, demanding execution of the treaty, or war would be declared. Part of her strategy against the Portuguese included forming an alliance with the Dutch whose aim was to break the Portuguese monopoly on the slave trade in Africa. She requested and received a regiment of Dutch soldiers. Queen Nzingha's apparent strategy was to defeat the Portuguese and to later expel the Dutch from her country. Consequently, Nzingha maintained friendly relations with the Dutch. She also sought an alliance with the Juga chief, Kasanji, by promising to marry him.

Aside from freeing her country from European control, Queen Nzingha sought to expand her kingdom from Matamba in the East to the Atlantic Ocean. In 1623, at the age of forty-one, she became the queen of Ndongo. She preferred to be called king, though, and when she led her regiments into battle, she supposedly dressed as a man. Nzingha also possessed feminine charm and was particularly good at maintaining both personal and political friends. She graciously rewarded both, and her friendships and alliances were hardly ever challenged.

In 1645, her sister, Fungi, was taken prisoner by the Portuguese and later beheaded. Queen Nzingha also suffered a series of military setbacks that year. Consequently, she began to examine her religion and compare her people's god (Tem-Bom Dumba) with the Christian God. She decided to subscribe once again to Christianity.

For the most part, Nzingha used her newly acquired religion as a political tool whenever it was advantageous. However, to demonstrate her sincerity, she set out to reform her people's customs, including the abolition of polygamy. At the age of seventy-five, she also provided an example for her constituents by marrying one of her courtiers. In 1657, when one of her chiefs spoke of attacking the Portuguese, she had him decapitated and sent his head to the Portuguese viceroy.

Near the end of Queen Nzingha's reign, she sent an emissary to the Pope requesting missionaries. She died on December 17, 1663, at the age of eighty-one and was buried in a Capuchin habit--as she had requested--with a crucifix and rosary in her hands.

After her death, Angola fell under Portuguese control. Queen Nzingha symbolized the epitome of resistance against European domination in Africa's interior. Although she failed to expel the Portuguese, she is remembered as one of the most important personalities in Angolan history.

OSEI TUTU
(Oh'-see Too'-too)
(1695–1717)

Tradition has it that Osei Tutu and his chief advisor and priest founded the Ashanti nation in 1695. At an assembly called by Osei Tutu, Anokye, his priest, caused a "Golden Stool" to fall from the heavens and rest on Tutu's knees. This Stool supposedly possessed the collective soul of the Ashanti people. Tradition further holds that Tutu was able to establish unity by forbidding people to speak of former customs and traditions. Thus, the Golden Stool represented unity to the Ashanti people.

Osei Tutu was probably born in the latter part of the seventeenth century. Legend surrounding his conception states that his uncle, Obiri Yeboa, the ruler of Kwaman, had only one sister who could not bear him an heir to the throne. In Ashanti society, succession was passed on to one's nephew. Obiri Yeboa sent his sister to a famous shrine, which was located in what is now the southeastern portion of present-day Ghana, to pray for the birth of a child. Thus, Osei Tutu was born and legend holds that he was named after the shrine.

The Ashanti Empire rose to power out of the Atlantic Slave Trade. Although the empire's early ascendancy was based on trading gold, the Ashanti soon realized that slave trading was a much more lucrative business. In the early 1600's the Ashanti Kingdom consisted of several small states located along the Volta River. These states were later unified in the latter part of the seventeenth century under Tutu's leadership. Tutu spent his younger days in Akan, a small kingdom located near the Volta and Pra River area. Their army was equipped with European weaponry, which they had exchanged for slaves and gold. By the early 1700's the Akan kingdom controlled at least 250 miles along the coastal area.

It was at Akan that Tutu learned military strategies and economic and political organizational skills that were attributed to the kingdom's greatness. In 1670, upon his uncle's death, Tutu returned home to succeed him to the throne. Osei Tutu then began to use his acquired military and organizational expertise to build the powerful Ashanti nation. To make the Ashanti union strong and enduring, he provided the new nation with the capital city of Kwaman (renamed Kumase), a yam festival, the Golden Stool, and a flexible constitution. He formed a political union with several neighboring tribes, and the chief of the Bretuo clan was accepted into the union as the second most important Ashanti. To strengthen his empire, Osei Tutu implemented a reward system by creating "service" stools. These stools were reserved for the treasurer, and the heads of the traders, silver and goldsmiths, and they were presented for faithful and meritorious service.

The Ashanti nation was mainly a military one, divided into six military divisions. In 1698, Tutu launched a campaign against his main adversary, the Denkyera, defeating them twice in 1701. In 1717, he launched a campaign against the Akyem Kotok, but his army was ambushed as it crossed the Pra River. Osei Tutu was struck by a bullet and killed, and his body was washed away.

Although his body was never located, his memory remained steadfast. Since it was believed that Osei Tutu perished on a Saturday, his people instituted their most sacred ceremonial oath to commemorate his tragic death. The event is referred to as the Coromantee Miminda (Coromantee Saturday); however, the oath was so sacred it was hardly ever mentioned by name, but was commonly referred to as "the great oath of the dreadful day."

As the first Asantehene (king), Osei Tutu more than tripled the area of the Ashanti and transformed it into a unified state. He is also credited with establishing the patterns for the empire's government and leadership, thereby making his empire one of the most famous of the West African forest kingdoms.

SHAKA
(Shah-kah')
(1813–1829)

Shaka (also known as Chaka), warrior-king of the Zulu, was born in 1787 to Senzangukon, a Zulu chieftain, and his lesser wife, Nandi. It is documented that because of Nandi's fierce temper, both she and Shaka were expelled from the royal court, and consequently Shaka was forced to live his childhood in humiliation. Thus, Shaka grew up with a strong determination to prove himself and to regain his royal status.

When Shaka was a young man, he served in the army of Dingiswayo (one of the most powerful rulers of Zululand) where Shaka's acts of bravery won him Dingiswayo's admiration. Upon Senzangukon's death, Dingiswayo saw an opportunity to establish his influence over the Zulu by giving Shaka, his protégé, the military assistance to ascend to power. Shaka is accused of killing his half-brother and seizing the throne. At that time, Shaka was only twenty-six and Zululand was only one hundred square miles in size. The new Zulu ruler declared it was his aim to rule all Africans. Shortly afterwards, Dingiswayo was killed by Zwide, another political aspirant. Shaka in turn set out to assassinate Zwide; after two attempts, Zwide was killed, though reportedly not by Shaka.

Shaka implemented a new system of military organization that incorporated regiments from defeated tribes. Accordingly, when a chiefdom was conquered it became a territorial segment of Shaka's kingdom-at-large. The young warriors became a part of his royal army and were drilled and fought beside combatants from other chiefdoms. This encouraged their loyalty to transcend the bounds of the warriors' original environment.

To maintain his royal army, Shaka established military towns and provided his army with the best of training and provisions. The Zulu king demanded the strictest of discipline and perfection from his regiments. For example, his soldiers were required to remain celibate during their period of enlistment. Any violation of this rule was punished by death. He also killed any soldier that exhibited signs of fear. Shaka's existence was based on excellence and he imposed his strict requirements on others.

Shaka also revolutionized the Zulu army's weaponry and its military tactics. He perfected several complex battle formations that outflanked and confused his enemies. It was customary for Zulu warriors engaged in battle to throw their spears and retreat. Shaka considered this method both unsatisfactory and cowardly. If his men retained their weapons and advanced right up to their enemies behind protective shields, Shaka reasoned the Zulus would have their foes at a considerable disadvantage. Shaka therefore designed a short handled stabbing spear, an "assegai," that was used and retained throughout battle.

Shaka unified many tribes of the South African region and his efforts are directly credited with saving that region from European domination during his lifetime. Nevertheless, some historians have characterized the Zulu ruler as an extremely militaristic man who was prone to violence. Ironically, in 1829 at the age of forty-two, Shaka met with a violent and premature death at the hands of his own brother. He was repeatedly stabbed to death, and his body was thrown to the vultures. Many Black contemporary historians believe that Shaka is perhaps the most misinterpreted of all the African kings.

MOSHESH
(Mo'-she-sh)
(fl. c. 1824–1870)

The tribal wars that swept over South Africa during the 1800's wiped out many small tribes. Consequently, many of the remaining victims sought refuge in the mountainous region of Lesotho. These tribes were provided protection by an African king named Moshesh in a stronghold called "Thaba Bosui" (Mountain of Night). In 1824, Moshesh and his 21,000 followers united to form Basutoland.

The exact date of Moshesh's birth is unknown, but it is believed that he was born in the late 1790's. During Shaka's reign, Moshesh was forced to flee to the mountains. The location for his stronghold was excellent for both hunting and farming. Not only were his people agriculturally inclined, they were also excellent horsemen. Aside from that, the mountains provided Moshesh with an excellent form of natural protection. The retreat was situated on a flat plateau 5,000 feet above sea level. Under Moshesh's leadership, the Basuto became relatively wealthy.

In 1836, the Boers (the Dutch Huguenots) and the British began to invade Moshesh's domain and small skirmishes developed. Despite the advanced weaponry of the Europeans, they proved to be no match for Moshesh and his followers. The African warrior was successful in running off their herds, and when the Europeans attempted to attack his people with cannons, Moshesh's followers retaliated by dropping huge boulders down on them, causing terrible avalanches.

In 1843, the British concluded a peace treaty with Moshesh; although Moshesh signed the treaty, he still had severe reservations regarding the final outcome of his contact with all Europeans. They were bitter enemies, but he figured that both the Boers and the British would someday unite against him. Moshesh was also quick to learn that religion played a major role in the White man's politics. As such, he introduced Christianity to his people and welcomed missionaries into his territories. This served to anger the Boers and to please the British.

Moshesh still worried that the White man would eventually treat him and his people as they had treated other tribes. Therefore, Moshesh attacked the Boers because he feared that they would eventually attack him. Subsequently, the British and the Boers united against him. Although Moshesh won many battles, he was wise enough to know that the strength and resources of the British Empire far outweighed his own. Accordingly, he wrote a letter to the Queen of England stating, "I beg peace from you. . . . Let it be enough I pray, and let me no longer be considered an enemy of the Queen. . . ." Shortly thereafter, the British pulled their forces from the area.

With the British gone, Moshesh then directed his efforts against the Boers and those native chiefs who opposed him. Although he was forced to fight with spears against the Boers, he won battle after battle. The war with the Boers raged for many years. At the age of eighty, Moshesh was still determined that his enemies would not conquer his territory. To ensure that the Boers would not be successful, before his death in 1870, Moshesh placed his people under the protection of the more distant enemy, the foe less able to raid the Basuto - - the British Empire.

Moshesh was praised as the man who outsmarted and defeated the Europeans. He was never beaten on the battlefield or in any acts of diplomacy. Mosesh was truly one of the greatest African statesmen of all time, for he possessed the qualities that make a great leader.

YAA ASANTEWA
(Yah Ah-san'-te-wah)
(1863–1923)

The deposition and exile of Ashanti ruler Prempeh I led to an uneasy peace and eventually to war in the early 1900's, when British Governor Sir Frederick Hodgson demanded that the Ashanti Kumase give him the "Golden Stool." Yaa Asantewa, the queen-mother of the Ashanti state of Ejisu, spearheaded the war in 1900 between the British and the Ashanti that is named after her.

Throughout the late 1800's, the British continued to press the Ashanti to accept British sovereignty. However, their ruler Prempeh I firmly refused and sent a delegation to England to present his position before the British Parliament. Because the British considered Prempeh the center of Ashanti resistance, they attempted to depose him by sending him into exile. Among those included in the exile was Asantewa's son, Afrane Kuma.

The Ashanti considered the British demand for the Stool insulting and sacrilegious. The British were ignorant of the fact that the Golden Stool was not a throne, but a scared object. To the Ashanti, the Golden Stool was the equivalent of the Ark of the Covenant. Even the Ashanti kings were not permitted to sit on it. The Golden Stool was considered one of the great masterpieces of African art. It was carved out of a solid block of teak and studded with golden nails and ornaments. Among these ornaments was the skull of King Adinkera of the Fanti. Tradition has it that the Stool fell from the skies. It was supposedly conjured by a magician so that the Ashanti nation would become very powerful. To the Ashanti, the Golden Stool represented wealth, courage, health, and strength. At ceremonial processions, the Stool was carried even ahead of the king. It was housed in a special building and was always guarded by two chiefs. The Golden Stool was linked with the destiny of their great nation. The British thought that once the sacred Stool was in their possession, it would break the spirit of the Ashanti and disunite them.

This was a period of political unrest for the Ashanti nation. In 1896, the British arrested King Kwasi Prempeh I, along with approximately thirty other dignitaries and deported them to the Seychelles Islands. Tensions were high on both sides, and matters worsened when Hodgson stated in clear-cut terms that their king would not be released soon.

Nana (Queen-Mother) Yaa Asantewa swore on the Great Oath of the Ashanti and called upon her people to support her in her quest against the British. It was bad enough that the British had insulted and deported their king; now they demanded the surrender of their most sacred possession. Supported by her people, Yaa Asantewa was appointed to lead the Ashanti into battle.

The war proved to be very bloody. Many British were captured and imprisoned in stockades. They suffered from hunger and thirst and consequently many of them died. Before the war was over, many of the Ashanti chiefs were captured and sent to join Prempeh I on the Seychelles Islands. Yaa Asantewa was also sent into exile.

In 1901, the Ashanti were finally defeated, and on January 1, 1902, the Ashanti nation was placed under the jurisdiction of the British governor of the Gold Coast. The Asantewa War was the last Anglo-Ashanti war. Although the Ashanti lost the war and Yaa Asantewa was captured, she is best remembered for her brave attempt to save her nation from further indignities. Queen Yaa Asantewa died in the Seychelles in 1923, before King Prempeh I was returned home.

MENELIK II
(Men'-el-lek)
(1889–1913)

Menelik II was Emperor of Ethiopia from 1889 to 1913. He was born Sahaba Mariem in August 1844 to Hayle Menekot, elder son of the Prince of Shoa, and Ejjegayehu, a commoner employed in the palace of Ankober. His father became king of the Shoa in 1847 and died in 1855, during the invasion of Shoa by Ethiopian Emperor Tewodros II (1847–1868). Menekot's loyal subjects named the young Sahaba the new king of the Shoa, but with Tewodros II in power, the title was a meaningless one.

After his father's death, Sahaba was captured by Tewodros and was raised by him. Tewodros treated the Shoa heir well and gave him his daughter in marriage, when he became of age. Sahaba escaped on July 1, 1865; he returned to Shoa, disposed of the ruler and became the negus (king) of Shoa. Sahaba was unsuccessful in his attempts at preventing Ras Kass (John IV) from gaining the throne. John IV later conducted a campaign against Sahaba to force him to accept his authority. Although John IV was victorious, he still feared Sahaba. Consequently Menelik and John IV entered into a political agreement. As such, Sahaba's daughter married one of John's sons, and Sahaba was declared heir to the throne. In 1889 John was killed at the battle of Metemma and Sahaba ascended the throne. He then changed his name to Menelik II, signifying his belief in his blood ties to Menelik I, Makeda's son.

Menelik II incorporated all the principalities of Shoa into his kingdom by military and peaceful means. He was an astute administrator and a capable military leader. He personally led many military campaigns and entrusted others to his generals. His dealings with nobility and the central government were generally successful. Only once did he fight against the central authority. Menelik organized his country into regions and provided each with its own governor, and in 1907, he patterned his central government after European models.

Menelik II was a genius at using foreign powers without permitting them to dominate his country. He welcomed European ambassadors, technicians, military experts, traders, and missionaries into his country. He was interested in innovations, trading, and the acquisition of modern weaponry. In 1889, he signed a treaty with Italy that later resulted in war. The war culminated in the defeat of the Italian army in 1896 and delayed the realization of Italy's imperialistic dreams in Africa. That same year, upon the death of Emperor Yohannes, who died as a result of wounds he had received in battle, Menelik proclaimed himself the emperor of Ethiopia. He was crowned Negusa-Nagast (King of Kings) on November 2, 1889. Most of the regional nobility supported him.

By 1899, Ethiopia had extended as far as Kenya in the south, Somaliland in the East, and the Sudan in the West. However, Ethiopia remained landlocked under his reign. He is credited with building several railroads, which linked Ethiopia with the outside world. During the last part of Menelik's reign, he devoted much of his time to construction projects including schools, hospitals, industries, and journalistic ventures.

In 1908, Menelik's health started to decline, after he suffered a series of strokes which eventually led to his death. Although the exact date of his death is in dispute, it is generally accepted that he died on the night of December 12/13, 1913. Menelik II was one of the greatest men in the history of modern Africa. Although he had no formal education, he doubled the territory of Ethiopia, consolidated the central authority and introduced modernization and improvement to Ethiopia.

HAILE SELASSIE
(Hal'-le Se-las'-se)
(1892 - 1975)

Emperor Haile Selassie is said to have been the 111th descendant of King Solomon and the Queen of Sheba. He ruled Ethiopia from 1930 to 1936 and from 1941 until 1974, when he was peacefully deposed. He is credited with modernizing Ethiopia.

He was baptized Haile Selassie (Might of the Trinity), but until his accession, he was known as Ras Tafari Makonnen. He was educated by tutors from the French mission and at the Menelik School. At the age of fourteen, Selassie so impressed Menelik II his great-uncle, that he was given the official court title of "dejazmatch" (commander of the door). In 1909, Menelik II, appointed Selassie as governor of Basso and of Harar in 1911. Also that year, Selassie married Menelik's great-granddaughter, and they had six children.

When Menelik died in 1913, he was succeeded by his grandson Lij Yasu. Three years later, Selassie successfully brought about Yasu's downfall. Menelik's daughter Zawditu was named empress, and Selassie became regent and heir to the throne. As such, Selassie's policies dominated those of Empress Zawditu. His efforts were directed at international recognition, expanded education, the abolishment of slavery, and the elimination of foreign intervention. To this end, Ethiopia joined the League of Nations in 1923. The following year, Selassie toured Jerusalem, Cairo, and Europe. His trips abroad added to his belief that Ethiopia should be modernized. He also emancipated slaves in 1924.

Upon the death of Empress Zawditu, Haile Selassie was crowned emperor on November 2, 1930. Shortly after being named emperor, Selassie introduced a written constitution, and he formed a parliament and appointed ministers. One of his primary concerns was maintaining a successful balance with France, Britain, and Italy. When the Italian army invaded Ethiopia in 1935, Selassie personally led his troops in battle. However, the Italians advanced on Addis Ababa in May 1936, and Selassie and his political advisors fled the country. On June 30, 1936, Selassie appealed to the world, in a memorable speech before the League of Nations, to impose military sanctions on Italy. He warned the League members that "God and history will remember your judgment." For almost five years he lived in exile in Bath, England. In 1940, he went to Sudan, where he helped organize a campaign that led to the defeat of Italy. He returned triumphantly to Ethiopia in May 1941.

Emperor Haile Selassie was very interested in educational reform. He founded both secondary and technical institutions, and he is also credited with founding the Haile Selassie I University. Further, he contributed large sums of his personal fortune to support higher education.

In 1955, on the 25th anniversary of his coronation, Haile Selassie revised Ethiopia's constitution to include voting privileges. During the 1960's, Haile Selassie supported African nationalism by helping establish the Organization of African Unity (OAU). He was also one of the mediators of the 1960's conflict between Algeria and Morocco. Because the standard of living of most of his subjects scarcely changed and efforts at land reform failed, his authority was challenged in an abortive coup in 1960. Consequently, improvements were made and Selassie promised to give more power to the parliament.

However, in 1973, Emperor Selassie was charged with corruption and inefficiency, and the famine caused by a severe drought led to increased criticism. At that time, Selassie appointed the progressive Endalkachew Mekonnen as prime minister. A committee was also selected to draft a new constitution. However, Selassie's efforts proved to be insufficient and in 1974, many of his advisors were executed and Emperor Selassie was put under house arrest during a coup by his army.

Selassie died on August 27, 1975, at the age of 83. His downfall brought the 3,000-year-old Solomonic dynasty to an end. He was buried without services at an unnamed location.

TEST YOURSELF

Now that you have familiarized yourself with our historic African Kings and Queens in this sixth series of Empak's Black History publications, this section, in three parts, MATCH, TRUE/FALSE, MULTIPLE CHOICE/FILL-IN, is designed to help you remember some key points about each notable African King or Queen. (Answers on page 32)

MATCH

I. *Match the column on the right with the column on the left by placing the appropriate alphabetical letter next to the King or Queen it represents.*

1. Makeda ______
2. Haile Selassie ______
3. Affonso I ______
4. Hatshepsut ______
5. Gudit ______
6. Piankhi ______
7. Nzingha ______

A) Wife of King Solomon
B) Female Pharaoh
C) King of Kush and Nubia
D) Mvemba Nzinga of Congo
E) Was called Ras Tafari
F) Converted to Catholicism
G) Founder of the Zagwe Dynasty

TRUE/FALSE

II. *The True and False statements below are taken from the biographical information given on each African King or Queen.*

1. Although Sunni Ali professed to be a Moslem, he held steadfast to traditional African religion. ______
2. It is documented that Jugurtha did not want to go to war. ______
3. Yaa Asantewa returned to the Ashanti in 1923. ______
4. Tuthmosis was one of the kings of the New Kingdom Period and a member of the XVIIIth Dynasty. ______
5. Osei Tutu founded the empire of Mali in 1695. ______
6. Mansa Musa had an army of over 100,000 soldiers. ______
7. Hatshepsut's greatest accomplishments were in religion. ______
8. Makeda was the mother of Haile Selassie. ______

MULTIPLE CHOICE/FILL-IN

III. *Complete the statements below by underlining the correct name, or by filling-in the correct answer which you have read in the biographical sketches.*

1. (Mansa Musa I, Menes, Menelik II) founded the ancient city of Memphis.
2. Nefertiti raised ______________________ and he married one of her daughters.
3. The Assyrians defeated (Taharqa, Yaa Asantewa, Affonso I).
4. ______________________ designed the assegai.
5. (Nefertiti, Nzingha, Haile Selassie) died in 1974 and was buried at an unnamed location.
6. ______________________ was educated in Carthage.
7. ______________________ was compared to the historic Joan of Arc.
8. (Tutankhamon, Askia Muhammad, Makeda) had a military title.
9. Modern Ethiopia was united by ______________________.
10. (Osei Tutu, Gudit, Jugurtha) attempted to sweep the Romans from Numidia.
11. (Moshesh, Piankhi, Massinissa) fought against the Boers and the British.

CROSSWORD PUZZLE

ACROSS

1. United Ethiopia
3. Welcomed the Portuguese to his country
5. Moslem king of Songhay Empire
6. 111th descendant of the Queen of Sheba
7. Ashanti ruler who established Golden Stool
10. Songhay ruler who lost his sight
13. Berber queen
15. Zulu warrior-king
16. War was named in her honor
17. United Upper and Lower Egypt
18. First woman pharaoh
19. Diplomatic Basuto king
20. War was named in his honor
21. Esato

DOWN

1. Numidian king who supported Rome
2. Was buried in a Capuchin robe
3. First pharaoh to preach monotheism
4. "The beautiful one"
8. His golden coffin was discovered in 1922
9. Nubian ruler who designed rock temple
11. Nubian king who conquered Egypt
12. European maps of West Africa
14. Hatshepsut was his co-regent
17. The Queen of Sheba

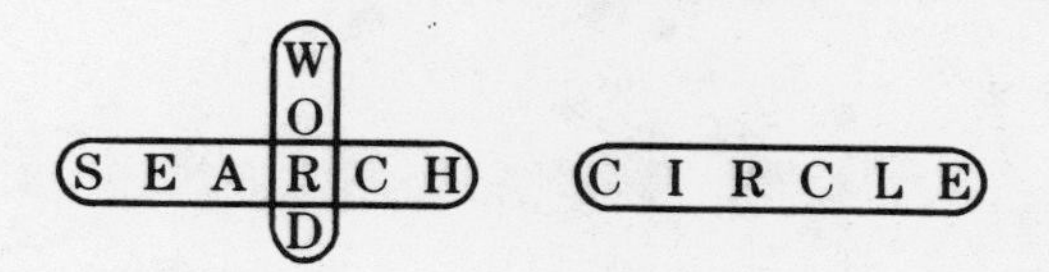

1. Affonso I
2. Akhenaton
3. Askia Muhammad
4. Dahia Al-Kahina
5. Gudit
6. Haile Selassie
7. Hatshepsut
8. Jugurtha
9. Makeda
10. Mansa Musa I
11. Massinissa
12. Menelik II
13. Menes
14. Moshesh
15. Nefertiti
16. Nzingha
17. Osei Tutu
18. Piankhi
19. Shaka
20. Sunni Ali Ber
21. Taharqa
22. Tutankhamon
23. Tuthmosis III
24. Yaa Asantewa

The names of our twenty-four AFRICAN KINGS AND QUEENS are contained in the diagram below. Look in the diagram of letters for the names given in the list. Find the names by reading FORWARD, BACKWARDS, UP, DOWN, and DIAGONALLY in a straight line of letters. Each time you find a name in the diagram, circle it in the diagram and cross it off on the list of names. Words often overlap, and letters may be used more than once.

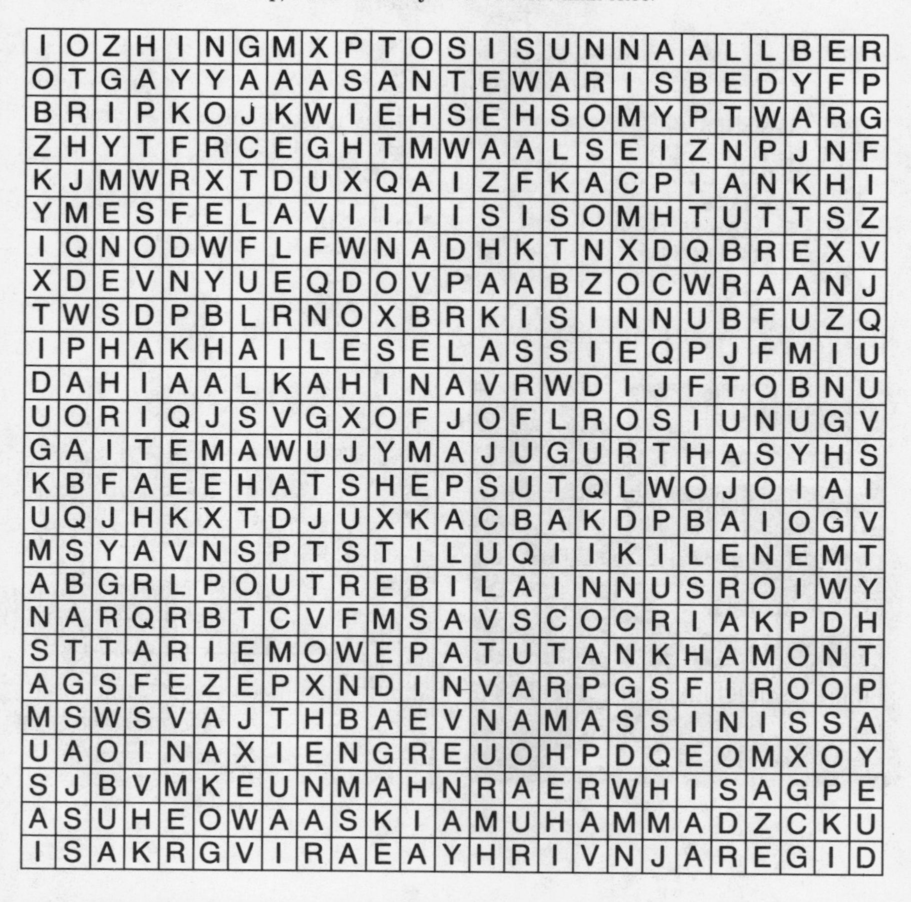

I	O	Z	H	I	N	G	M	X	P	T	O	S	I	S	U	N	N	A	A	L	L	B	E	R
O	T	G	A	Y	Y	A	A	A	S	A	N	T	E	W	A	R	I	S	B	E	D	Y	F	P
B	R	I	P	K	O	J	K	W	I	E	H	S	E	H	S	O	M	Y	P	T	W	A	R	G
Z	H	Y	T	F	R	C	E	G	H	T	M	W	A	A	L	S	E	I	Z	N	P	J	N	F
K	J	M	W	R	X	T	D	U	X	Q	A	I	Z	F	K	A	C	P	I	A	N	K	H	I
Y	M	E	S	F	E	L	A	V	I	I	I	I	S	I	S	O	M	H	T	U	T	T	S	Z
I	Q	N	O	D	W	F	L	F	W	N	A	D	H	K	T	N	X	D	Q	B	R	E	X	V
X	D	E	V	N	Y	U	E	Q	D	O	V	P	A	A	B	Z	O	C	W	R	A	A	N	J
T	W	S	D	P	B	L	R	N	O	X	B	R	K	I	S	I	N	N	U	B	F	U	Z	Q
I	P	H	A	K	H	A	I	L	E	S	E	L	A	S	S	I	E	Q	P	J	F	M	I	U
D	A	H	I	A	A	L	K	A	H	I	N	A	V	R	W	D	I	J	F	T	O	B	N	U
U	O	R	I	Q	J	S	V	G	X	O	F	J	O	F	L	R	O	S	I	U	N	U	G	V
G	A	I	T	E	M	A	W	U	J	Y	M	A	J	U	G	U	R	T	H	A	S	Y	H	S
K	B	F	A	E	E	H	A	T	S	H	E	P	S	U	T	Q	L	W	O	J	O	I	A	I
U	Q	J	H	K	X	T	D	J	U	X	K	A	C	B	A	K	D	P	B	A	I	O	G	V
M	S	Y	A	V	N	S	P	T	S	T	I	L	U	Q	I	I	K	I	L	E	N	E	M	T
A	B	G	R	L	P	O	U	T	R	E	B	I	L	A	I	N	N	U	S	R	O	I	W	Y
N	A	R	Q	R	B	T	C	V	F	M	S	A	V	S	C	O	C	R	I	A	K	P	D	H
S	T	T	A	R	I	E	M	O	W	E	P	A	T	U	T	A	N	K	H	A	M	O	N	T
A	G	S	F	E	Z	E	P	X	N	D	I	N	V	A	R	P	G	S	F	I	R	O	O	P
M	S	W	S	V	A	J	T	H	B	A	E	V	N	A	M	A	S	S	I	N	I	S	S	A
U	A	O	I	N	A	X	I	E	N	G	R	E	U	O	H	P	D	Q	E	O	M	X	O	Y
S	J	B	V	M	K	E	U	N	M	A	H	N	R	A	E	R	W	H	I	S	A	G	P	E
A	S	U	H	E	O	W	A	A	S	K	I	A	M	U	H	A	M	M	A	D	Z	C	K	U
I	S	A	K	R	G	V	I	R	A	E	A	Y	H	R	I	V	N	J	A	R	E	G	I	D

QUIZ & GAME ANSWERS

MATCH

1.–A
2.–E
3.–D
4.–B
5.–G
6.–C
7.–F

TRUE/FALSE

1.–TRUE
2.–TRUE
3.–FALSE
4.–TRUE
5.–FALSE
6.–TRUE
7.–FALSE
8.–FALSE

MULTIPLE CHOICE/FILL-IN

1.–MENES
2.–TUTANKHAMON
3.–TAHARQA
4.–SHAKA
5.–HAILE SELASSIE
6.–MASSINISSA
7.–DAHIA AL-KAHINA
8.–ASKIA MUHAMMAD
9.–MENELIK II
10.–JUGURTHA
11.–MOSHESH

CROSSWORD PUZZLE

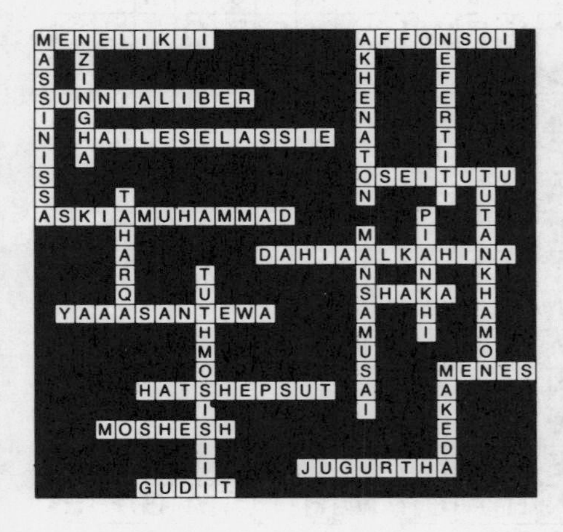

WORD SEARCH

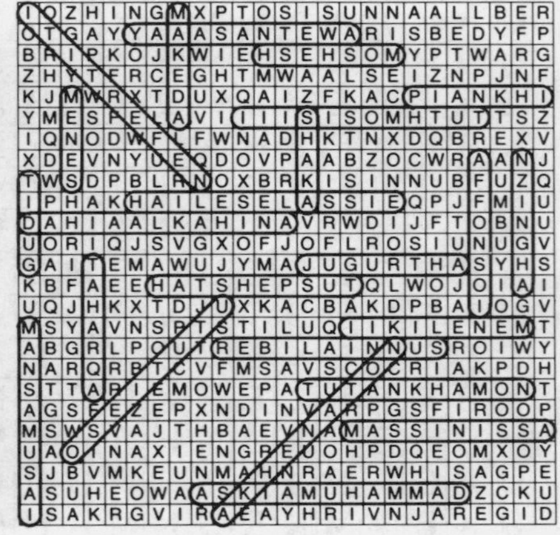

Send to: Empak Publishing Company, 212 E. Ohio St., Suite 300, Chicago, IL 60611—Phone: (312) 642-8364

EPC

Name ______________________

Affiliation ______________________

Address ______________________
P. O. Box numbers not accepted, street address must appear.

City ______________ State ________ Zip ________

Phone# (______)______________ Date ________

Method Of Payment Enclosed: ( ) Check ( ) Money Order ( ) Purchase Order

Prices effective 10/1/93 thru 8/31/94

ADVANCED LEVEL

Quantity	ISBN #	Title Description	Unit Price	Total Price
	0-9616156-0-5	"A Salute to Historic Black Women"		
	0-9616156-1-3	"A Salute to Black Scientists & Inventors"		
	0-9616156-2-1	"A Salute to Black Pioneers"		
	0-9616156-3-X	"A Salute to Black Civil Rights Leaders"		
	0-9616156-4-8	"A Salute to Historic Black Abolitionists"		
	0-9616156-5-6	"A Salute to Historic African Kings & Queens"		
	0-9616156-6-4	"A Salute to Historic Black Firsts"		
	0-9616156-7-2	"A Salute to Historic Blacks in the Arts"		
	0-9616156-8-0	"A Salute to Blacks in the Federal Government"		
	0-922162-00-X	"A Salute to Historic Black Educators"		

INTERMEDIATE LEVEL

Quantity	ISBN #	Title Description	Unit Price	Total Price
	0-922162-75-1	"Historic Black Women"		
	0-922162-76-X	"Black Scientists & Inventors"		
	0-922162-77-8	"Historic Black Pioneers"		
	0-922162-78-6	"Black Civil Rights Leaders"		
	0-922162-80-8	"Historic Black Abolitionists"		
	0-922162-81-6	"Historic African Kings & Queens"		
	0-922162-82-4	"Historic Black Firsts"		
	0-922162-83-2	"Historic Blacks in the Arts"		
	0-922162-84-0	"Blacks in the Federal Government"		
	0-922162-85-9	"Historic Black Educators"		
	Total Books		❸ Subtotal	
			❹ IL Residents add 8.75% Sales Tax	
		SEE ABOVE CHART	❺ Shipping & Handling	
			❻ Total	

GRADE LEVEL: 4th, 5th, 6th

KEY STEPS IN ORDERING

❶ Establish quantity needs.
❷ Determine book unit price.
❸ Determine total cost.
❹ Add tax, if applicable.
❺ Add shipping & handling.
❻ Total amount.

BOOK PRICING • QUANTITY DISCOUNTS

❶ Quantity Ordered	❷ Unit Price
1-49	$2.09
50 +	$1.77

❺ SHIPPING AND HANDLING

Order Total	Add
Under $5.00	$1.50
$5.01-$15.00	$3.00
$15.01-$35.00	$4.50
$35.01-$75.00	$7.00
$75.01-$200.00	10%
Over $201.00	6%

In addition to the above charges, U.S. territories, HI & AK, add $2.00. Canada & Mexico, add $5.00. Other outside U.S., add $20.00.